AF575860

EARLE RICE JR.

Mitchell Lane
PUBLISHERS
2001 SW 31st Avenue
Hallandale, FL 33009
www.mitchelllane.com

Printing 1 2 3 4 5 6 7 8

ABOUT THE COVER: An Islamist militant, masked and garbed in black, stands atop a Middle Eastern mosque. In a triumphant gesture, he brandishes a Kalashnikov AK-47 against a backdrop of a black Islamist flag and villagers gathered for a funeral below.

ABOUT THE AUTHOR: Earle Rice Jr. is a former senior design engineer and technical writer in the aerospace, electronic-defense, and nuclear industries. He has devoted full time to his writing since 1993, specializing in military and counterinsurgency subjects. Earle is the author of more than 80 published books. He is listed in *Who's Who in America* and is a member of the Society of Children's Book Writers and Illustrators, the League of World War I Aviation Historians, the Air Force Association, and the Disabled American Veterans.

Library of Congress Cataloging-in-Publication Data
Names: Rice, Earle, author.
Title: Islamic State / by Earle Rice Jr.
Description: Hallandale, FL : Mitchell Lane Publishers, [2018] | Series: Terror INC | Includes bibliographical references and index.
Identifiers: LCCN 2017009130 | ISBN 9781680200553 (library bound)
Subjects: LCSH: IS (Organization)—Juvenile literature. | Terrorism—Religious aspects—Islam—Juvenile literature. | Terrorism—Middle East—Juvenile literature.
Classification: LCC HV6433.I722 I85724 2017 | DDC 363.3250956—dc23
LC record available at https://lccn.loc.gov/2017009130

eBook ISBN: 978-1-68020-056-0

Contents

Words in **bold** throughout can be found in the Glossary.

Foreword

Terror has plagued the world since men in caves flailed away at each other with sticks and stones. As the world emerged from **primeval** times and entered the ancient age, humans clashed on a larger, more advanced scale called warfare. Slings, arrows, and spears wrought havoc in the Golden Age of Greece and stained the glory that was Rome. Ethnic and religious strife followed close behind. In medieval times, crusading Christians and faith-based Muslims carved a bloody path across the Middle East with sword, lance, and scimitar in the causes of God and Allah. Americans engaged in "total war" for the first time during the Civil War, a war pitting brother against brother and fathers against sons at a cost of 750,000 lives. The 20th century introduced global wars that claimed the lives of tens of millions of combatants and civilians.

Today, international terrorism has become a form of warfare. The U.S. Department of Defense defines terrorism as "the unlawful use of—or threatened use of—force or violence against individuals or property to **coerce** or intimidate governments or societies, often to achieve political, religious, or ideological objectives." In many parts of the world, terror is a way of life. Militant Muslim extremists seek to rid Muslim countries of what they view as the **profane** influence of the West and replace their governments with fundamentalist regimes based on their interpretation of the religion of **Islam**.

The American way of life changed forever when 19 Islamist terrorists flew fuel-laden aircraft—flying bombs—into the World Trade Center in New York City and the Pentagon in Washington,

The vast majority of the world's Muslims disavow terrorism and the corruption of their religion by jihadist militants. On July 14, 2005, these Muslims of Leeds, England, gathered in Millennium Square to honor the victims of a London bombing a week earlier. They joined millions of others across Europe in a tribute marked by two minutes of silence. Leeds is the home city of the suspected suicide bombers.

DC, on September 11, 2001. Today, radical Islamist groups continue to be America's main threat of terrorism.

It should be noted that only a small minority of Muslims believe in terror as a strategy. A recent Gallup poll indicated that just seven percent of the world's 1.6 billion Muslims support extremist views of terrorism. The purpose of this book is to alert and enlighten the reader about that seven percent, while affirming the essential righteousness of the other 93 percent of Islam's followers. Peace be upon the gentle of mind, spirit, and deed.

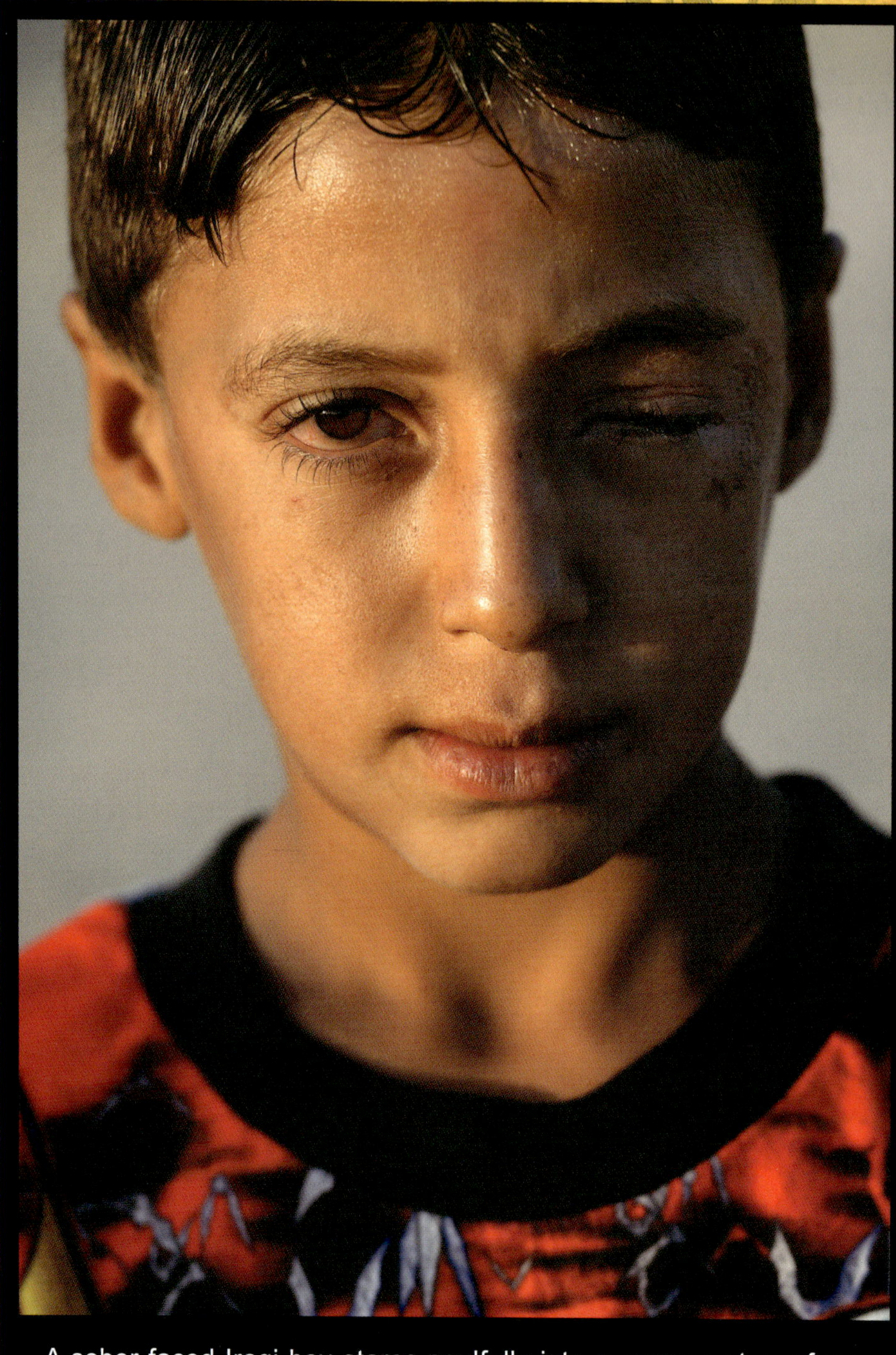

A sober-faced Iraqi boy stares soulfully into a camera at a refugee camp near Mosul. The loss of his left eye bears witness to the savage fighting for Mosul, as Iraqi forces battled to recapture Iraq's second-largest city from Islamic State insurgents in December 2016.

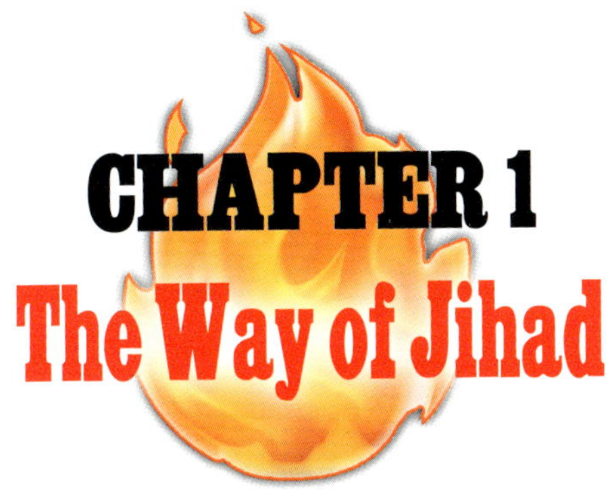

CHAPTER 1
The Way of Jihad

Theirs is a story of great courage and even greater faith. It happened in 2014 in a small village outside Baghdad, Iraq. They were four Iraqi Christians under the age of 15. They were perhaps too young to understand the depth of their conviction—or what was about to happen to them. Islamic State (IS) terrorists were holding them captive under the threat of death. They had offered the children one last chance to save themselves.

"You say the words that you will follow **Muhammad**," their captors said.

"No, we love Yasua [Jesus]," the children replied. "We have always loved Yasua. We have always followed Yasua. Yasua has always been with us."

"Say the words!" their captors demanded.

"No, we can't do that," the children said.

The terrorists chopped off all their heads.[1]

Given the choice of converting to Islam or death by beheading, four brave Christian children refused to renounce their faith. Anglican priest Andrew White told their story in an interview shown in a Christian Broadcast Network video.

White, known as the "Vicar of Baghdad," asked, "How do you respond to that?" He answered his own question. "You just cry. They are my children. That is what we have been going through. That is what we are going through."[2]

By way of further example, White told of an Iraqi Christian man pressured to convert to Islam by an Islamic State militant. "You say the words of conversion or we will kill all of your

children,"[3] threatened the militant. Desperate to spare his children, the man said the words.

Afterward, **distraught** over his coerced conversion, the Iraqi man telephoned White seeking some measure of comfort. "I said the words [of conversion]," he told the priest, "Does that mean Yasua doesn't love me anymore? I have always loved Yasua. I said those words because I couldn't see my children killed."[4]

"Jesus still loves you," the priest replied. "He will always love you."[5]

These tragic tales speak to the havoc wrought by terrorists of the Islamic State across vast expanses of Iraq and Syria in recent years. Of the seemingly endless number of terror groups operating around the world today, IS claims the dubious distinction of being the strongest and deadliest of them all. Speaking in July 2014, U.S. State Department official Brett McGurk said IS is "worse than al-Qaeda" and "is no longer a terrorist organization . . . it is a full-blown army."[6]

By mid-October 2014, according to the U.S. Central Intelligence Agency (CIA), IS likely commanded up to 31,000 fighters in Iraq and Syria. This number represents three times as many fighters as previously feared. Moreover, IS forces are equipped with advanced weapons systems and vehicles. These include tanks, armored personnel carriers, field artillery, self-propelled howitzers, and multiple-rocket launchers. Additional IS weaponry includes anti-tank guided missiles, anti-aircraft guns, and a limited number of portable air-defense systems.

Soviet D-44 85 mm field cannon

Islamist militants train in the sand and brush with AK-47s and rocket launchers. They typically wear all-black masks and attire to create a sense of dread in their adversaries.

As its numbers and this advanced array of equipment indicate, IS is clearly not just another terrorist organization. Rather, it is indeed "a full-blown army." Yet, until early 2014, most Americans had never heard of the Islamic State. To many, it seemed as if IS suddenly appeared on the world scene from out of nowhere. But IS did not just *appear*, it evolved. So, what exactly is IS, many Americans might ask, and where did it come from?

IS, or the Islamic State, was previously known as ISIS, or the Islamic State in Iraq and Syria. It also went by the name of ISIL, or the Islamic State in Iraq and the Levant. (In common usage, the Levant encompasses the eastern shores of the Mediterranean Sea and consists of Cyprus, Lebanon, the Palestinian territories, Israel, Jordan, and southern Syria.) By definition, the IS is an unrecognized Islamist state that claims, by right of conquest, areas of eastern Syria and northern and western Iraq. These areas in total are about the size of Belgium. It is also a self-proclaimed caliphate (the dominion of a **caliph**) that claims worldwide religious authority over all Muslims.

The Islamic State documented its goals in a statement published in 2014. As reported by the *Christian-Muslim News Digest*, these goals are to "expand the dominion of Islam across numerous borders in the region, enforce traditional Islamic law, and defeat God's 'enemies,' which through this and subsequent statements seem to include **Shia** Muslims, Arab nationalists, the Muslim Brotherhood, Jews, Christians, and Yezidies."[7] (Yezidies are a Kurdish ethno-religious community whose origin dates back many centuries.) IS later circulated a map outlining a five-year plan to bring much of the Middle East, North Africa, broad areas of Asia, and even some parts of Europe under its control.

Most scholars believe that the Islamic State originated as an offshoot of al-Qaeda, the militant Islamic group founded by Osama bin Laden in the late 1980s. Some analysts say that Ansar

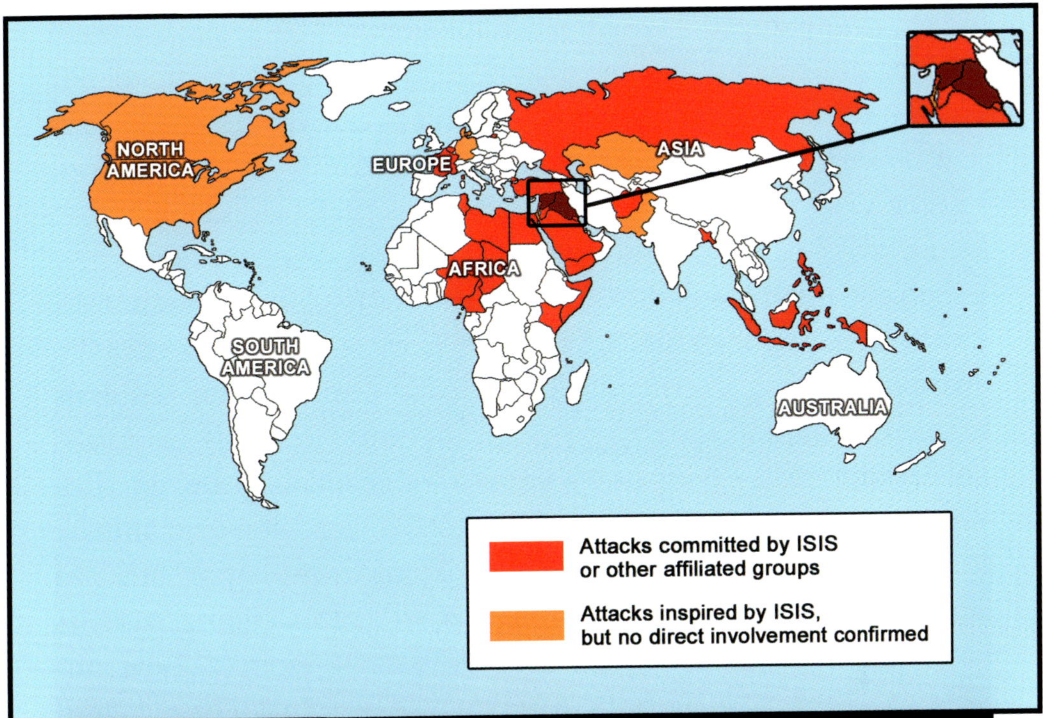

This map illustrates terror attacks linked to IS beginning in January, 2013 and continuing through April, 2017. These attacks have killed thousands of people and wounded many thousands more. The area in dark red—primarily Iraq and Syria—shows where IS has gone beyond attacks and actually controls territory.

al-Islam (Partisans of Islam), a **Sunni** extremist group, was the predecessor of IS. In either case, the birth of the Islamic State extends back to at least 1999. And Abu Musab al-Zarqawi was its father.

Born in Zarqa, Jordan, as Ahmad Fadhil Nazzal al-Khalaylah, he later renamed himself. He dropped out of high school and took to the streets as a petty criminal, involved in nearly 40 run-ins with the police.

In 1989, at the age of 23, Zarqawi traveled to Afghanistan to become a mujahideen ("holy warrior"). The mujahideen had been

Abu Musab al-Zarqawi, leader of al-Qaeda in Iraq (AQI), discusses strategy with a masked associate. In this video—seized by U.S. forces during a raid on a terrorist safe house in Iraq—Zarqawi is later shown, to his embarrassment, having difficulty operating a U.S. machine gun.

fighting a **jihad** ("holy war") against the Soviet-backed Afghan government for a decade. But he arrived too late. The Soviets were already withdrawing. He worked instead for a brief time for Al-Bonian al-Marsous, a small jihadist newspaper.

In an interview with Mary Anne Weaver for *The Atlantic* magazine, an Afghan jihadist offered an early appraisal of Zarqawi. "Zarqawi arrived in Afghanistan as a zero," he said, "a man with no career, just floundering about. He trained and fought and he came back to Jordan with ambitions and dreams: to carry the **ideology** of jihad. . . . It's not so much what Zarqawi did in the jihad—it's what the jihad did for him."[8]

Mujahideen

Mujahideen

Mujahid is an Arabic term meaning "one who strives in the path of God." Mujahideen is the plural of mujahid, which derives from the same Arabic root as jihad, "to strive or struggle." Jihad is often defined as a "holy war." So mujahideen are frequently referred to as "holy warriors." The terms date back many years. The modern use began in the nineteenth century when Afghan tribesmen battled British soldiers seeking to control their country.

In December 1979, Soviet troops invaded Afghanistan to lend support to the recently installed, Soviet-friendly communist regime of Babrak Karmal. Devout Muslims bitterly resented the far-reaching land and social reforms initiated by the new government. Both urban and rural groups rebelled against the government. The **insurgency** spread across the country.

The Soviets viewed the mujahideen as outlaws. On the other hand, the United States saw them as "freedom fighters." So the U.S. aided the mujahideen with weapons and supplies in their fight against Soviet forces. The Afghan mujahideen fought the Soviets to a standstill, forcing their withdrawal in 1989.

Today, the term "mujahideen" is freely applied to any Muslim group engaged in hostilities with non-Muslims or other Muslims considered to have abandoned Islam.

Radical Jordanian cleric Abu Qatada (right) confers with Islamist scholar Sheik Abu Muhammad al-Maqdisi on September 24, 2014, shortly after Qatada's release from a prison near Amman, Jordan.

CHAPTER 2
A Serious Jihadist

Probably the most important thing the jihad did for Abu Musab al-Zarqawi was to bring him together with Sheikh Abu Muhammad al-Maqdisi. Born in Nablus in the West Bank of Palestine, Maqdisi is a Jordanian-Palestinian writer and jihadi theorist. He is also a militant Salafist cleric. **Salafism** is an Islamic religious movement that originated in Egypt at the end of the nineteenth century. It rejects modern practices and calls for a return to a strict interpretation of the **Quran** and related Islamic principles.

"It's not surprising that Zarqawi embraced Salafism," said Jarret Brachman, a counterterrorism expert whom the U.S. government often consults. "Jihadi Salafism is black and white—and so is everything that Zarqawi's ever done."[1]

In 1993, Zarqawi and Maqdisi left Afghanistan and returned to Jordan. Maqdisi set out on a speaking tour of the country. Meanwhile, Zarqawi put together a small Islamist group of a dozen or so men. Maqdisi was one of them. Originally called *al-Tawhid* (One God), the group was later renamed as *Bayat al-Imam* (Allegiance to the Imam). Its chief aim was to overthrow the Jordanian monarchy. They would replace it with a government based on Islamic principles.

The new revolutionaries soon proved themselves inept. In 1994, Maqdisi smuggled seven grenades into Jordan and handed them over to Zarqawi for safekeeping. Zarqawi found a hiding place for the weapons in the basement of his family's home. The ruse didn't fool Jordanian intelligence agents. They had already been observing Maqdisi and quickly discovered the grenades. Zarqawi claimed he had found them in the street. The judges realized he was lying. They convicted the two men of possessing illegal weapons. They were also convicted of being members of an illegal organization and sentenced to 15 years in prison.

In the 1980s, Zarqawi had already spent a brief jail term for drug possession and sexual assault. He easily adapted to life in Jordan's Swaqa prison. Under Maqdisi's direction, he memorized all 6,236 verses of the Quran. He spent the rest of his free time bodybuilding and recruiting fellow inmates to his cause.

"Zarqawi was the muscle, and al-Maqdisi the thinker," observed Abdullah Abu Rumman, a journalist who was in prison at the same time as Zarqawi. "He was extremely protective of his followers, and extremely tough on prisoners outside his group. He didn't trust them. He considered them infidels [nonbelievers]."[2]

In May 1999, Jordan's newly enthroned King Abdullah II declared a general **amnesty**. Zarqawi was released. But he again found himself under surveillance by government security agents. They suspected him of terrorist activities. To avoid being arrested, he fled. He carried a letter of introduction from Abu Kutaiba al-Urduni, a well-known Jordanian jihadi leader. The letter was addressed to Osama bin Laden, the founder of al-Qaeda.

Zarqawi arrived back in Afghanistan in December. He soon met with bin Laden in the southern city of Kandahar. "It was loathing at first sight,"[3] a former Israeli intelligence officer said. Bin Laden disliked Zarqawi's crudeness, and his hatred of Shias and willingness to kill them. (Bin Laden's mother was a Shia.) Zarqawi held firm to his belief that all Shias should be executed. And he refused to accept bin Laden as his leader. Moreover, Zarqawi wanted to focus on the "near enemy" in the area known as al-Sham, or so-called "un-Islamic" governments in the Levant.

On the other hand, bin Laden preferred focusing his attacks on the "far enemy" (primarily the United States and Israel).

Al-Qaeda leaders debated the issue. Eventually they decided to provide Zarqawi with enough money to establish a training camp. It was located close to the Iranian border, in the desert near the western Afghan city of Herat—as far away from bin Laden as possible. Early in 2000, Zarqawi set out for the site, along with a handful of followers. In Herat, Zarqawi formed the militant organization *Jund al-Sham* (Soldiers of the Levant). He planned to build a force capable of fighting anywhere in the world. Over the next 18 months, his fighters multiplied from dozens to hundreds. During this period, bin Laden summoned Zarqawi to Kandahar at least five times to pledge allegiance to him. Zarqawi declined every time. He didn't believe that either bin Laden or al-Qaeda were serious jihadists.

Al-Qaeda leader Osama bin Laden (left) sits with his second-in command Dr. Ayman al-Zawahiri for an interview with Pakistani journalist Hamid Nir in November 2001. The doctor served as a translator for Osama bin Laden.

On October 7, 2001, less than a month after the 9/11 terrorist attacks, the United States attacked Afghanistan. Zarqawi had little choice but to join forces with al-Qaeda for the first time. He and his Jund al-Sham fighters fought in and around Herat and Kandahar. But they had to flee to Iran within two months. From Iran, Zarqawi moved to the Kurdish areas of northern Iraq. Soon after the U.S. invasion of Iraq in 2003, he moved again to the Sunni strongholds of central Iraq. He established a base in Ramadi where he recruited new followers from among Iraq's Sunni minority.

Zarqawi announced his arrival in Iraq with a blast on August 19. He orchestrated a truck bombing of the UN headquarters in Baghdad that killed High Commissioner for Human Rights Sergio Vieira de Mello and 21 others. President George W. Bush condemned the bombing: "The terrorists have again shown their contempt for the innocent. . . . The civilized world will not be intimidated."[4]

Two months later, Zarqawi followed up on his attack on the UN headquarters. He launched a carefully choreographed series of simultaneous car-bomb attacks on the International Red Cross headquarters and five police stations in Baghdad. The synchronized attacks claimed the lives of 35 people and injured 244 more.

British foreign secretary Jack Straw received news of the terrorist bombings while attending a meeting of the European Union (EU) in Brussels. Reacting with "shock and outrage," he said the attack on the Red Cross "shows the depth of **depravity** to which they stoop."[5] Zarqawi would soon stoop even deeper into the depths of depravity.

A Simple Man

Abu Musab al-Zarqawi

The terrorist known as Abu Musab al-Zarqawi was born as Ahmed Fadeel Nazal al-Khalayleh. His father was a retired soldier and a respected elder in the Bani Hassan tribe, one of Jordan's largest clans. Zarqawi took his nom de guerre, or pseudonym, from his hometown of Zarqa, a dusty mining town 17 miles north of the Jordanian capital Amman. Despite a strict Islamic upbringing, he shunned religion as a youth and built a reputation as a juvenile delinquent.

Because Zarqawi was a shadowy figure, much of his life remains cloaked in the obscure or unknown. Government wanted posters listed his height and weight as "unknown." His mastery of disguise and false passports added to his mystique. He was so secretive that even many of his cohorts did not know what he looked like. Much of what is known about him comes from conflicting accounts of supporters and enemies, making it hard to separate fact from fiction.

Though loyal to his friends, Zarqawi was quick to fight when crossed. "Al-Zarqawi was a simple, but a dangerous man," said Yousef Rababaa, one of Zarqawi's fellow inmates for three years at Swaqa prison. "You just don't come near him if you don't buy his **bigoted** gospel."[6]

A black-masked Iraqi insurgent, with one eye peering at the camera, displays a wanted poster offering a reward for information leading to the capture of al-Qaeda operative Abu Musab al Zarqawi. U.S. aircraft dropped many such leaflets on the volatile city of Fallujah in July 2004. Translated from the Arabic, the poster reads "Al-Zarqawi . . . he is only hurting your families, children, friends and innocent people by his terrorist acts. If you have any information about him or other terrorists then call the numbers below and you might get a reward."

CHAPTER 3
Sheikh of the Slaughterers

Abu Musab al-Zarqawi's campaign of suicide bombings across Iraq soon elevated him to superstar status in the world of international jihadists. Graphic violence became his calling card. His acts of raw brutality repulsed most onlookers in the West. But many in the Islamic world regarded Zarqawi as an avenger of decades of humiliation and abuse suffered by Muslims. Accounts and images of him and his terrorist activities spread rapidly across the media.

"Zarqawi loved the limelight, and his was an easy face to hate," said former CIA officer Bruce Riedel, a counterterrorism expert. "But the fact was that an easy face for us to hate made him attractive to so many other people."[1]

One of the chief aims of most militant Islamists is to drive all Westerners and other nonbelievers out of Muslim lands. Zarqawi was no exception. With this goal in mind, he set out to strike fear in the ultimate enemy. He upped his terror tactics against Americans and other Westerners in Iraq with a succession of kidnappings and beheadings.

Nicholas Berg, a radio-tower repairman from West Chester, Pennsylvania, became the first victim in May 2004. A five-and-a-half-minute video went viral across the Internet. It began with Berg seated in front of five jihadists. All were dressed in black, wearing ski masks and *shemaghs* (scarves). Berg, wearing an orange jumpsuit much like those worn by U.S. prisoners, introduced himself with brief details of his family and background. In an article written for *New York* magazine, Jonathan Hayes, a New

York City medical examiner, described what happened next: "One of the men reads in Arabic for much of the tape, the tension increasing as he plows on and on with his **manifesto**. He stops, then cries out 'God is great!' and they fall on Berg."[2] He was beheaded. The CIA later confirmed that the executioner was Zarqawi himself.

Hayes dissects dead bodies for a living. The nature of his work is not for the squeamish. He wishes he had not watched the video.

Zarqawi's group, now named *al-Tawhid wal Jihad* (**Monotheism** and Jihad), claimed responsibility for Berg's beheading. They said it was in retaliation for American abuses of Muslim captives in Baghdad's Abu Ghraib prison.

The next month, al-Tawhid wal Jihad coordinated a series of bombing attacks on security forces in Baghdad, Baqubah, Mosul, Fallujah, and Ramadi. The attacks killed more than 100 people, including three U.S. soldiers, and wounded 320 more. American officials linked the bombings to Zarqawi.

Zarqawi's campaign of violence in Iraq gained worldwide notoriety, not least in the secret headquarters of al-Qaeda. Despite their differences in aims and policy, Osama bin Laden invited Zarqawi to join forces with al-Qaeda. Zarqawi accepted, and pledged allegiance to bin Laden. In a statement issued on October 17, Zarqawi said, in part: "We shall, with great fury, instill fear in the enemies of Islam, who consider that through their war in Iraq they have nearly uprooted Islam from its recent stronghold. For this, we will turn [the war] into a hell for them."[3]

Zarqawi rebranded his group as *Tanzeem Qaedat al-Jihad Fi Bilad al-Rafidayn* (Base of the Jihad in the Country of the Two Rivers [Iraq]) and stepped up his campaign against U.S. and Iraqi targets. The United States designated his group—better known as al-Qaeda in Iraq (AQI)—a Foreign Terrorist Organization (FTO). They also offered a $25,000,000 bounty for his capture. On

December 28, bin Laden conferred upon Zarqawi the title of "**Emir** of al-Qaeda in the Country of Two Rivers" and urged all jihadis to follow and obey him.

Despite al-Qaeda central's new alliance with AQI, Zarqawi's brutal tactics earned the displeasure of bin Laden and his chief lieutenant, Ayman al-Zawahiri, over the next six months. In a letter in July, 2005, Zawahiri outlined al-Qaeda's objectives and called for Zarqawi not to lose sight of those goals. In the most polite terms, he urged Zarqawi to put aside his hatred toward Shia Muslims and focus on forcing the Americans and their Western allies out of Iraq. Zarqawi ignored Zawahiri's counseling and continued to wreak violence and barbarity across Iraq, particularly against the Shias.

Zarqawi believed attacks on Shias were necessary to create a sectarian divide and prod Sunni Muslims into fighting for their own liberation. In defense of Muslims killing Muslims, he said in an Internet audio, "[T]he killing of a number of Muslims whom it is forbidden to kill is undoubtedly a grave evil; however, it is permissible to commit the evil—indeed, it is even required—in order to ward off an even greater evil, namely, the evil of suspending *jihad*."[4] Guided by such dubious reasoning, Zarqawi slaughtered countless numbers of Shias, many by beheading. His barbarism earned him the fitting title of "The Sheikh of the Slaughterers."

In November, Zarqawi revisited his Jordanian homeland and coordinated bombing attacks on three Western hotels in the capital city of Amman—the Grand Hyatt Hotel, the Radisson SAS Hotel, and the Days Inn. The bombings killed 60 people and injured 115 others. Back in Iraq, a bombing attack in February 2006 on the al-Askari Mosque in the city of Samarra severely damaged the Shia holy site. It set off a Shia retaliation that took more than a thousand lives.

In the spring of 2006, an intensive intelligence operation tracked Zarqawi to a safe house north of Baghdad. Late in the evening of June 7, two U.S. F-16s targeted the house with a pair of guided bombs, destroying it. Zarqawi was pulled alive from the rubble. He died minutes later—but his movement lived on.

A car bomb attack left this scene of destruction in a market in the Iraqi capital of Baghdad in June 2006. The attack killed 10 people and wounded 25 others. A newspaper in the forefront of the photograph carries a picture and story of the recently killed al-Qaeda in Iraq (AQI) leader Abu Musab Zarqawi.

Zarqawi's Legacy

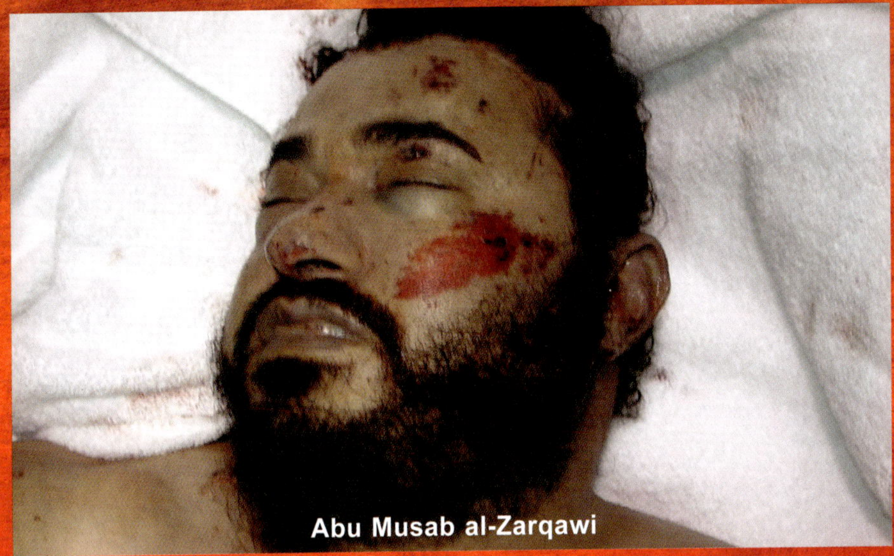

Abu Musab al-Zarqawi

At the time of his death, many people viewed Abu Musab al-Zarqawi as the most feared figure in Iraq. *The New York Times* once described him as "[p]erhaps the most ferocious embodiment of *takfiri* Salafism today."[5] A *takfiri* is a Muslim who accuses another Muslim of apostasy—abandonment of one's religion. Salafism calls for restoring Islam to its original pure state. Zarqawi viewed all Shias as **apostates**. His strategy for the restoration of Islam began with the elimination of all apostates and infidels (nonbelievers). After the United States invaded Iraq in 2003, Zarqawi initiated a campaign of mass attacks against Shias and Shia holy shrines. He fomented sectarian tensions that pitted Sunni insurgents against Shia death squads and turned Iraq into a killing field. Oddly enough, his savage methods attracted thousands of Sunni foreign fighters eager to join in sectarian **genocide**.

Though Zarqawi was sometimes compared to Osama bin Laden, many authorities feel that the comparison was misleading. French investigator and researcher Jean-Charles Brisard writes, "You can't compare him to Osama bin Laden . . . al-Zarqawi has his own tactics, whose pillars are violence, chaos, and destruction."[6] Those three pillars will long be remembered as Zarqawi's legacy.

At a news conference held in April 2010, Iraqi Prime Minister Nouri al-Maliki holds a leaflet displaying photographs of Abu Omar al-Baghdadi, a man identified as the al-Qaeda leader in Iraq. Al-Maliki announced the deaths of both Abu Omar al-Baghdadi and Abu Ayyub al-Masri. As confirmed by U.S. military officials, U.S. and Iraqi forces killed both al-Qaeda leaders in a nighttime rocket attack on a safe house near Tikrit.

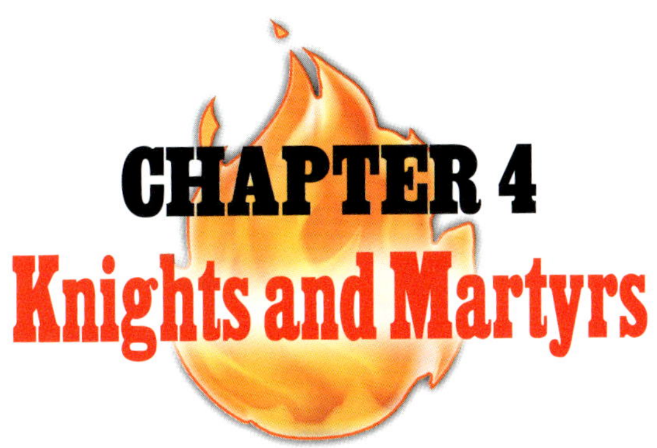

CHAPTER 4
Knights and Martyrs

Five days after the death of Abu Musab al-Zarqawi, al-Qaeda in Iraq announced that Abu Ayyub al-Masri was its new leader. Masri, also known as Abu Hamza al-Muhajir, was an Egyptian-born jihadist and former senior aide to Zarqawi. He had close ties to al-Qaeda's leadership and was a master bomb maker and explosives expert.

To make his presence felt right away, Masri personally beheaded two captive U.S. soldiers. Their bodies were mutilated and booby-trapped. AQI added, "We give the good news . . . to the Islamic nation that we have carried God's verdict by slaughtering the two captured crusaders [soldiers]."[1] The brutal slayings served notice that Zarqawi's legacy lived on with his successor.

In October 2006, al-Qaeda in Iraq merged with several other insurgent groups and called itself the Islamic State of Iraq (ISI). At this point, the group's leadership became murky. Supposedly, Abu Omar al-Baghdadi was named leader of ISI, and Masri assumed the post of ISI's war minister. However, numerous sources maintain that Abu Omar was a fictitious character made up by Masri so it would look like an Iraqi was the leader. Al-Qaeda in Iraq had become dominated by foreign fighters and was sometimes accused of being a puppet of foreign powers. Masri wanted to change the image of the newly formed ISI. So he installed an actor in the role of ISI's leader.

As ISI's war minister, Masri swore allegiance to the "made-up" leader Abu Omar al-Baghdadi. As U.S. General Kevin Bergner pointed out later, Masri "was essentially swearing allegiance to

himself, since he knew that Baghdadi was fictitious and totally his own creation."[2] Over the next few years, U.S. and Iraqi officials reported Baghdadi's death or capture several times. The reports turned out to be unfounded. Whether Abu Omar was real or fake remains an open question.

The Islamic State of Iraq functioned as a loose umbrella grouping of different tribal groups and Islamist brigades, including al-Qaeda in Iraq and the Mujahideen Shura Council (MSC).

ISI exhibited more forward thinking than AQI. While Zarqawi had concentrated on consolidating power and defeating enemies at hand, ISI took a more mature organizational approach. It directed its attention to the future of the war, the group, and Iraq. It established a full cabinet with ministry positions. And it drafted a constitution for post-invasion Islamist Iraq. At the same time, it still embraced the earlier objectives of Zarqawi. Its chief aims continued to be to expel foreign interests from Iraq, overthrow the current government, and replace it with an Islamic regime.

Al-Qaeda in Iraq continued its founder's brutal attacks. Its savagery backfired and led to the formation of the National Council for the Salvation of Iraq, or the *Sahwa* (Awakening) Movement. Writes military contractor Carter Andress:

> The Bedouin tribes of western Iraq . . . turned on al-Qaeda in Iraq, as the terrorist group became more extreme; their kidnappings for ransom and their assassinations were especially hateful to tribal members. . . . During the final throes of the battle for Ramadi, the *Sahwa* or Awakening rose up in what had become the ultimate safe haven in Iraq for the radical jihadis: the austere Sunni desert cities and villages of al Anbar.[3]

Together with General David Petraeus's "surge of an additional 20,000 U.S. troops in June 2007," the *Sahwa*—also known as the Anbar Awakening—signaled "the beginning of the end of the al-Qaeda-led insurrection in Iraq."[4]

By 2008, AQI's militant capability was drastically reduced. In early 2010, U.S. and Iraqi forces concluded that they had either captured or killed 34 of the top 42 AQI leaders. Though AQI continued to conduct occasional attacks throughout 2010 and 2011, it no longer posed a serious threat to Iraqi or coalition forces.

In a joint operation on April 18, 2010, U.S. and Iraqi forces raided a safe house near Tikrit where Abu Ayyub al-Masri was staying. They killed Masri, his assistant, and Abu Omar al-Baghdadi—or whoever was playing his role—and his son.

At a news conference, Iraqi Prime Minister Nouri al-Maliki announced the deaths of Masri and Baghdadi and produced photographs of their bloody corpses. Because of numerous earlier reports of Baghdadi's death, some observers doubted the latest report.

ISI removed all doubts of their deaths with a statement a week later: "After a long journey filled with sacrifices and fighting falsehood and its representatives, two knights [Masri and Baghdadi] have dismounted to join the group of **martyrs**. We announce that the Muslim nation has lost two of the leaders of jihad, and two of its men who are only known as heroes on the path of jihad."[5]

A month later, ISI announced that Abu Bakr al-Baghdadi was its new leader. According to intelligence reports, his real name is Ibrahim Awwad Ibrahim al-Badri, also known as Abu Du'a. Baghdadi had been serving as supervisor of the group's **Sharia** committee and member of its senior consultative council. Whether ISI appointed him leader or he appointed himself remains unclear.

Born near Samarra, Iraq, in 1971, Baghdadi is known to be pious and scholarly. He earned a PhD in Islamic studies from Baghdad's Islamic University. He may also hold degrees in history

Abu Bakr al-Baghdadi, leader of the Islamic State, addresses his followers in 2014. The reach of his extremist group extends from his self-proclaimed caliphate in Syria and Iraq to Libya, northeast Nigeria, Afghanistan, and beyond.

and Arab linguistics. Though he kept a low profile for years, his tactical shrewdness and ruthlessness as a military leader soon earned him international recognition and notoriety.

In August 2011, ISI pledged to carry out 100 attacks across Iraq in retaliation for the death of Osama bin Laden at the hands of U.S. Navy SEALs. Baghdadi set in motion a varied campaign of raids, suicide attacks, roadside bombs, and small arms attacks in all Iraqi cities and rural areas.

Two months later, the U.S. State Department listed Baghdadi as a Specially Designated Global Terrorist—and he was just getting started.

The Surge

General David Petraeus (second from left) tours a neighborhood in Baqubah, Iraq. American forces had retaken the area in early July, 2007 as part of the surge authorized by President George W. Bush.

In March 2003, the United States and its coalition allies invaded Iraq. Their stated mission was to disarm Iraq of weapons of mass destruction, topple the dictatorial regime of Saddam Hussein, and free the Iraqi people. The initial phase of the operation toppled Saddam in 21 days. It then shifted into eight years of almost continuous warfare against Islamic insurgents.

In January 2007, after experiencing large losses and increasing violence in Iraq, the United States adopted a new strategy to fight the insurgents. President Bush authorized a temporary increase in the number of U.S. troops by more than 20,000. The new strategy became known as the "surge." It was directed by U.S. generals David Petraeus and Ray Odierno. After heavy initial losses, the level of violence declined.

The surge was greatly aided by the Sunni "Awakening" movement. Sunni tribesmen who had formerly fought against U.S. troops realigned themselves to counter the increasingly brutal insurgents of al-Qaeda in Iraq and others.

Though the surge was controversial, it is generally credited with suppressing the major fighting in Iraq and stabilizing the country. In 2011, after failing to reach an agreement over the legal immunity of U.S. troops from Iraqi law, President Barack Obama withdrew all American troops.

Two al-Nusra Front fighters stand by an automatic sniper rifle. The foreign-built rifle operates by remote control. Al-Nusra Front was formed in January 2012. Since then, its militants have operated at the forefront of the fighting in Syria. It has established itself as the most aggressive and effective force in the Syrian Civil War. Its militants consistently operate at the forefront of the fighting. The United States designated the group as a foreign terrorist organization in December 2012.

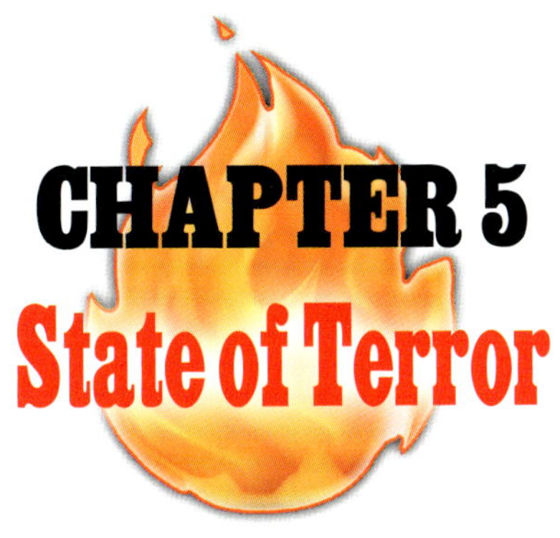

CHAPTER 5
State of Terror

In November 2007, General Joseph Fil, the U.S. commander for Baghdad, had warned, "Al-Qaeda [in Iraq], though on the ropes, is not finished by any means. They could come back swinging if they're allowed to."[1] Over the ensuing years, several circumstances came together to allow AQI—and later ISI—to "come back swinging." Of these, the chief factors were, arguably, the political instability caused by the withdrawal of U.S. forces, the radicalization of the region following the start of the Arab Spring late in 2010, and the onset of the civil war in Syria in 2011.

Added to these enabling factors were the continuing rift between the Sunnis and the Shias and the disbanding of *Sahwa* forces. Iraqi Prime Minister Nouri al-Maliki, a Shia, failed to merge the *Sahwa* fighters into the regular army as he had promised. As a result, they had nowhere to go in a job-deprived Iraqi economy. Many joined ISI and other Islamist groups. Other Sunnis who felt they would never get a fair deal from Maliki also boosted ISI's recruiting efforts.

When the fighting began in Syria in March 2011, ISI leader Abu Bakr al-Baghdadi was quick to seize on the potential for expansion there. He sent Abu Muhammad al-Julani to Syria to organize jihadist cells in the region. Julani formed the al-Nusra Front (or *Jabhat al-Nusra*) in July. It was funded and supplied by ISI and foreign donors. Al-Nusra quickly became a prominent opposition force in the fight against Bashar al-Assad's regime. Unlike its ISI patron, it avoided brutal executions and sectarian attacks. But it did impose religious (Sharia) laws in areas it con-

trolled. The United States designated al-Nusra a terrorist organization in December 2012.

In April 2013, Baghdadi released a recorded audio message. It claimed that the al-Nusra Front was an extension of the Islamic State of Iraq. Baghdadi further announced the merging of the two groups under the name of Islamic State of Iraq and al-Sham (ISIS). Al-Sham variously refers to Syria or the Levant. So the name was alternately given as Islamic State of Iraq and Syria (ISIS) or Islamic State of Iraq and the Levant (ISIL).

Julani conceded ISI's help in getting started but flatly denied the merger. Instead, he renewed his allegiance to al-Qaeda leader Ayman al-Zawahiri. Zawahiri ruled against the merger. Baghdadi rejected Zawahiri's ruling and announced he was going ahead with the merger. In the tangled web of insurgencies, the two groups fought each other on some occasions, with each side incurring heavy losses. At other times, they fought together.

By the start of 2014, ISIS had become one of the most ruthless and influential rebel groups operating in Syria. It numbered several thousand fighters operating on both sides of the Syrian-Iraqi border. A spokesman for the group said its growing success was due to God's will. "The state has not prevailed by numbers, nor equipment, nor weapons, nor wealth," he said, "rather it prevails by Allah's bounty alone, through its creed."[2]

The creed of ISIS is pretty basic and not unlike the ideology of numerous other Islamic jihadists: Return Islam to a purer earlier form, establish a worldwide caliphate, and convert or kill all infidels. ISIS fighters have also declared their intentions to destroy Israel. Baghdadi himself, once briefly imprisoned by U.S. forces, told his captors upon his release, "I'll see you guys in New York."[3]

After carrying out attacks across the borders of Iraq and Syria throughout 2013, ISIS made its first major gains early in 2014. ISIS fighters stormed into the Iraqi cities of Fallujah and Ramadi. Both cities had seen bloody street-to-street fighting during the

In a dazzling display of smoke and fireworks, an explosion rocked the Syrian city of Kobani in October 2014. Islamic State militants claimed responsibility for the suicide car bomb attack on the People's Protection Unit (YPG)—Kurdish fighters positioned in the city's center. Spectators viewed the spectacular burst from the outskirts of the Turkish border town of Suruc, in Sanliurfa province. The government of Turkey subsequently allowed Kurdish fighters to cross the Syrian border to advance their fight against Islamic State insurgents attacking Kobani. The U.S. military aided the Kurdish defenders with airdrops of ammunition and medical supplies.

U.S.-led invasion of 2003 and afterward. ISIS claimed control of Fallujah on January 7 and fought off Iraqi attempts to reclaim it in an intense three-week battle.

In February, after months of in-fighting between ISIS and al-Nusra Front, Ayman al-Zawahiri publicly disavowed ISIS. Baghdadi ignored Zawahiri's **disavowal** and defied his orders to keep the Iraq and Syria Islamist movements separate. In an audio recording, he expressed his ultimate goal in an enthusiastic shout-out to all Muslims:

> So to arms, to arms, soldiers of Islam, fight, fight. Rush O Muslims to your state. It is your state. Syria is not for Syrians and Iraq is not for Iraqis. The land is for Muslims, all Muslims. . . . If you hold to it you will conquer Rome and own the world, if Allah wills.[4]

Baghdadi's words clearly showed his international intentions that not only posed a threat to all Catholics—whose historical seat is Rome—but also to the world at large.

The ISIS war machine rolled on in the spring of 2014, gathering strength in numbers, in captured weaponry, and in stolen funds. In June, ISIS fighters seized the Iraqi cities of Mosul and Tikrit and the border town of al-Qaim.

Soon afterward, ISIS announced the creation of a caliphate in the Syrian and Iraqi territory under its control. It further proclaimed Baghdadi as its emir, with authority over the world's estimated 1.6 billion Muslims. Henceforth, the announcement stated, ISIS would be known simply as the Islamic State (IS).

On August 8, President Obama, in opposition to a new terrorist state in Syria-Iraq, authorized limited air strikes against the militants. He also ordered a slow buildup of U.S. ground forces in Iraq.

IS captured the attention of all Americans with the savage videotaped beheading of U.S. journalist James Foley on August 19. IS called it a message to the USA. Two weeks later, an IS video showed a similar beheading of Steven Sotloff, another U.S. journalist. Additional beheadings followed.

On September 11, 13 years after the 9/11 attacks on the World Trade Center, President Obama announced a four-part plan to "degrade and ultimately destroy"[5] IS. It was later named Operation Inherent Resolve. The plan called for air strikes in Iraq and Syria, increased support to ground forces in the region, counterterrorism activities, and humanitarian aid to civilians. Critics dismissed the plan as potentially taking too long and ultimately insufficient to defeat IS militants.

In an October 6 interview with USA TODAY's Susan Page, former CIA director Leon Panetta appraised the IS situation. "I think we're looking at kind of a 30-year war,"[6] he said. The Iraqis began to fight back the following year, regaining control of Tikrit in April, but losing the city of Ramadi to IS fighters in May. Then, in the fall of 2015, fortune began to frown on the Islamic State.

Russia entered the civil war in Syria in October in support of the Assad regime. It began mounting airstrikes, not only against IS militants but also against al-Qaeda-linked terrorists and U.S.-backed rebel groups. Iraqi forces, aided by U.S. air support, recaptured Fallujah the following June. By the end of 2016, the Iraqis had recaptured the eastern half of Mosul, Iraq's second-largest city, and about a quarter of IS-held territory in Iraq.

A U.S. Air Force drone pilot performs a preflight check on a MQ-1B Predator at a secret air base in the Persian Gulf region in January 2016. The Predator is an unmanned aerial vehicle (UAV) used by U.S. and coalition forces to launch airstrikes against Islamic State militants in Iraq and Syria. Cargo and troops are also distributed from this undisclosed location to support Operation Inherent Resolve (code name for the U.S. campaign against the Islamic State).

Even as the Islamic State was losing battles and territory in Iraq and Syria, it was exporting terror abroad. Since declaring itself a caliphate in June 2014, IS conducted or inspired more than 140 terrorist attacks in 29 countries in addition to Iraq and Syria. In the United States, two shooters in San Bernardino, California, killed 14 people and wounded another 21 at a Christmas party in 2015. A lone shooter in Orlando, Florida, killed 49 people at a nightclub and wounded dozens more in 2016. In both cases the shooters dedicated their acts to IS. Such attacks have claimed the lives of at least 2,000 victims and wounded thousands more.

As the world entered 2017, newly elected U.S. President Donald J. Trump vowed to destroy the Islamic State and rid the world of Islamic terror. He did not reveal how he planned to accomplish that goal. But one thing is certain—his task will not be easy.

On the night of June 16, 2016, a Saturday, Omar Mir Seddique Mateen attacked patrons of the Pulse nightclub in Orlando, Florida, killing 49 people and wounding 53 others in a mass shooting. Amid the massacre, Mateen phoned the police and pledged his allegiance to the Islamic State. Grieving citizens formed an impromptu memorial for the victims soon after the slayings.

Evil Aims

Though it was actually several years in the making, the Islamic State seemed to explode upon the world scene almost overnight. In the year 2014 alone, it morphed from a ragtag terror group into the strongest, fiercest, best-armed, best-equipped, and best-financed jihadist militia in the world. It seized control of a vast swath of Syrian and Iraqi territory estimated at somewhere between 12,000 and 35,000 square miles. And IS was just getting started.

In June 2014, when it proclaimed itself a caliphate, the Islamic State flooded the Internet with chilling images of what appeared to be its five-year plan for expansion. The plan extended its Syria-Iraq caliphate throughout the Middle East and North Africa, into Europe—Spain, Austria, and the Balkans—and even across western Asia to China. Such grandiose ambitions pose a threat to the West and to all who cherish liberty.

At the start of 2017, according to the U.S. National Counter-terrorism Center, the Islamic State was thought to operate in 18 countries around the world, including Afghanistan and Pakistan. It also found evidence of wannabe branches in Mali, Egypt, Somalia, Bangladesh, Indonesia, and the Philippines. Adding to the IS spread of terror, it claimed attacks in numerous countries in 2016, including Turkey, Indonesia, Belgium, France, Germany, the United States, and Bangladesh.

The UN estimates that the number of civilian deaths in Iraq since August 2014 now exceeds 20,000. In Syria, according to the Syrian Observatory for Human Rights, more than 300,000 people—including 86,000 civilians—have been killed since March 2011. Much of this senseless slaughter can be laid at the feet of the IS terrorists—and the carnage will continue until nations of the world band together and put an end to it.

TIMELINE

1979 Soviet troops invade Afghanistan in December.

1989 Abu Musab al-Zarqawi travels to Afghanistan to become a mujahideen. Soviets withdraw their forces.

1993 Zarqawi leaves Afghanistan and returns to Jordan.

1994 Zarqawi is sentenced to 15 years in prison for possessing illegal weapons.

1999 Zarqawi is released from prison on a general amnesty and returns to Afghanistan.

2000 Zarqawi forms militant organization Jund al-Sham in Herat training camp.

2001 U.S. launches air war against al-Qaeda and Taliban in Afghanistan on October 7.

2003 U.S. invades Iraq. Zarqawi orchestrates truck bombing in Iraq; coordinates synchronized attacks.

2004 Zarqawi beheads Nicholas Berg and justifies violence against Shias. Al-Tawhid wal Jihad launches a series of bombing attacks on security forces. Zarqawi pledges allegiance to Osama bin Laden. Bin Laden names Zarqawi "Emir of al-Qaeda in the Country of Two Rivers."

2005 Ayman al-Zawahiri outlines al-Qaeda goals and urges Zarqawi to rein in violence. Zarqawi coordinates three bombing attacks on Western hotels in Amman, Jordan.

2006 Al-Askari Mosque in Samarra is bombed. U.S. air attack kills Zarqawi in a safe house north of Baghdad. Al-Qaeda in Iraq announces Abu Ayyub al-Masri as its new leader. Al-Qaeda in Iraq merges with several other insurgent groups and rebrands itself as the Islamic State of Iraq (ISI).

2007 General David Petraeus's surge begins in June.

2008 AQI's militant capability is drastically reduced.

2010 U.S. and Iraqi forces raid a safe house near Tikrit and kill Abu Ayyub al-Masri and Abu Omar al-Baghdadi. ISI announces Abu Bakr al-Baghdadi as its new leader.

2011 Civil war begins in Syria in March. Abu Muhammad al-Julani forms al-Nusra Front in Syria. ISI pledges to carry out 100 attacks across Iraq in retaliation for the death of Osama bin Laden in August. U.S. State Department lists Baghdadi as a Specially Designated Global Terrorist. President Barack Obama withdraws all American troops from Iraq in December.

2012 U.S. designates al-Nusra a terrorist organization.

2013 Baghdadi claims al-Nusra Front is an extension of the Islamic State of Iraq; Julani denies merger, renews allegiance to al-Qaeda.

2014 Ayman al-Zawahiri publicly disavows ISIS. ISIS announces the creation of a caliphate in Syrian and Iraqi territory; rebrands itself as the Islamic State. IS beheads two Americans. President Obama announces a four-part plan to destroy IS. Leon Panetta warns of a protracted war.

2015 Iraqi forces recapture Tikrit from IS, lose Ramadi, then recapture it six months later. Russia begins air strikes against IS in Syria.

2016 Iraqi army and Shia militias recapture Fallujah. Eastern half of Mosul falls to Iraqi forces in December.

2017 IS attacks on two Egyptian Coptic churches on Palm Sunday kill more than 40 worshippers.

CHAPTER NOTES

Chapter 1 The Way of Jihad

1. Mark Andrews, "Before Beheading, Children Tell ISIS: 'No, We Love Jesus'." *Charisma News*. December 2, 2014. http://www.charismanews.com/world/46330-before-beheading-children-tell-isis-no-we-love-jesus
2. Ibid., p. 2.
3. Ibid.
4. Ibid.
5. Ibid.
6. Charles Lister, "Profiling the Islamic State." Brookings Doha Center Analysis Paper. Number 13, November 2014, p. 30. https://www.brookings.edu/wp-content/uploads/2014/12/en_web_lister.pdf
7. "Muslims React to Islamic State's Declaration of a Caliphate." *Christian-Muslim News Digest*. Issue 1(22) 2014. http://nifcon.anglicancommunion.org/media/110070/NIFCON-Digest-1-2014.pdf
8. Mary Anne Weaver, "The Short, Violent Life of Abu Musab al-Zarqawi." *The Atlantic*. Edited for the Web. June 8, 2006, p. 5. http://www.theatlantic.com/magazine/archive/2006/07/the-short-violent-life-of-abu-musab-al-zarqawi/304983/

Chapter 2 A Serious Jihadist

1. Mary Anne Weaver, "The Short, Violent Life of Abu Musab al-Zarqawi." *The Atlantic*. Edited for the Web. June 8, 2006, p. 6. http://www.theatlantic.com/magazine/archive/2006/07/the-short-violent-life-of-abu-musab-al-zarqawi/304983/
2. Ibid., p. 7.
3. Ibid., p. 9.
4. "Truck bomb kills chief U.N. envoy to Iraq." CNN. August 20, 2003. http://www.cnn.com/2003/WORLD/meast/08/19/sprj.irq.main
5. "Up to 40 die in Baghdad attacks." *The Guardian*. October 27, 2003. http://www.theguardian.com/world/2003/oct/27/iraq
6. "Seeds of al-Zarqawi army sown during prison term." *Lubbock Avalanche-Journal*. January 10, 2005. http://lubbockonline.com/stories/011005/wor_011005066.shtml

Chapter 3 Sheikh of the Slaughterers

1. Joby Warrick, "ISIS, with gains in Iraq, close in on founder Zarqawi's violent vision." *The Washington Post*. June 14, 2014. https://www.washingtonpost.com/world/national-security/isiss-gains-in-iraq-fulfill-founders-violent-vision/2014/06/14/921ff6d2-f3b5-11e3-914c-1fbd0614e2d4_story.html?utm_term=.3b632d52374d
2. Jonathan Hayes, "Second Opinion: A New York City medical examiner watches the video of Nick Berg's beheading and wishes he'd looked away." *New York* Magazine. May 31, 2004. http://nymag.com/nymetro/news/columns/witness/9183/
3. Jeffrey Pool, trans., "Zarqawi's Pledge of Allegiance to al-Qaeda: From Mu'asker al-Battar, Issue 21." Terrorism Monitor, Volume: 2, Issue: 24. December 15, 2004. https://jamestown.org/program/zarqawis-pledge-of-allegiance-to-al-qaeda-from-muasker-al-battar-issue-21-2/

4. Nimrod Raphaell, "'The Sheikh of the Slaughterers': Abu Mus'ab Al-Zarqawi and the Al-Qaeda Connection." MEMRI. Inquiry & Analysis Series Report No. 231. July 1, 2005, p. 6. https://www.memri.org/reports/%E2%80%98-sheikh-slaughterers%E2%80%99-abu-musab-al-zarqawi-and-al-qaeda-connection

5. Nir Rosen, "Iraq's Jordanian Jihadis." *The New York Times*. February 19, 2006. http://www.nytimes.com/2006/02/19/magazine/iraq.html?pagewanted=all&_r=0

6. "Seeds of al-Zarqawi army sown during prison term." *Lubbock Avalanche-Journal*. January 10, 2005. http://lubbockonline.com/stories/011005/wor_011005066.shtml

Chapter 4 Knights and Martyrs

1. "Al-Qaeda says new leader 'beheaded' kidnapped US soldiers." *The Scotsman*. June 17, 2006. http://www.scotsman.com/news/world/al-qaeda-says-new-leader-beheaded-kidnapped-us-soldiers-1-1122725

2. Charles River Editors, *The Islamic State of Iraq and Syria: The History of ISIS/ISIL* (Cambridge, MA: Charles River Editors, 2014), ch. 2.

3. Carter Andress, with Malcolm McConnell, *Victory Undone: The Defeat of al-Qaeda in Iraq and Its Resurrection as ISIS* (Washington, DC: Regnery Publishing, 2014), p. 50.

4. Ibid.

5. Charles River Editors, *Islamic State*, ch. 2.

Chapter 5 State of Terror

1. Mark Kukis, "Bracing for an al-Qaeda Comeback." *Time*. November 7, 2007. http://content.time.com/time/world/article/0,8599,1681443,00.html

2. Charles River Editors, *The Islamic State of Iraq and Syria: The History of ISIS/ISIL* (Cambridge, MA: Charles River Editors, 2014), ch. 2.

3. Jay Sekulow, with Jordan Sekulow, Robert W. Ash, and David French. *The Rise of ISIS: A Threat We Can't Ignore* (New York: Howard Books, 2014), p. 39.

4. Ibid., p. 40.

5. "Timeline: How Islamic State put itself on a collision course with the West." ABC News. October 3, 2014. http://www.abc.net.au/news/2014-10-03/islamic-state-a-timeline-of-escalating-terror/5788816

6. Susan Page, "Panetta: '30-year war' and a leadership test for Obama." *USA TODAY*. October 6, 2014. http://www.usatoday.com/story/news/politics/2014/10/06/leon-panetta-memoir-worthy-fights/16737615/

PHOTO CREDITS: Cover design elements: Bram Janssens/Dreamstime.com, StanOd/iStock/Getty Images Plus, Natis76/Dreamstime.com, and Sharon Beck; Interior design elements—Jupiterimages/liquidlibrary/Getty Images Plus, malija/iStock/Getty Images Plus, macrovector/iStock/Getty Images Plus, prudkov/iStock/Getty Images Plus, estherpoon/iStock/Getty Images Plus, and Sharon Beck. Photos: Cover, p. 1—Warrick Page/Stringer/Getty Images News; p. 3—Yorrico/Dreamstime.com; p. 5—Christopher Furlong/Staff/Getty Images News; p. 6—Carl Court/Staff/Getty Images News; p. 8—Bukvoed/cc by-sa 3.0; p. 9—Abid Katib/Stringer/Getty Images News; p. 11—Szabi237/cc by-sa 4.0; p. 12—Handout/Handout/Getty Images News; p. 13—Erwin Lux/cc by-sa 3.0; p. 14—REUTERS/Majed Jaber/Alamy Stock Photo; p. 17—Hamid Mir/cc by-sa 3.0; p. 19—Getty Images/Handout/Getty Images News; pp. 20, 24—REUTERS/Ali Jasim/Alamy Stock Photo; p. 25—PD-USGov-Military-Army; p. 26—Handout/Handout/Getty Images News; p. 30—World History Archive/Alamy Stock Photo; p. 31—Chris Hondros/Staff/Getty Images News; p. 32—Medyan Dairieh/ZUMA Wire/ZUMAPRESS.com/Alamy Live News/Alamy Stock Photo; p. 35—Gokhan Sahin/Stringer/Getty Images News; p. 37—John Moore/Staff /Getty Images News; p. 38—Spencer Platt/Staff/Getty Images News.

PRINCIPAL PEOPLE

Bashar al-Assad (bah-SHAHR al-AH-sahd)—President of Syria since 2000.

Abu Bakr al-Baghdadi (AH-boo buh-KAR al-bag-DAD-ee)—Caliph of the Islamic State.

Abu Omar al-Baghdadi (AH-boo OH-mahr al-bag-DAD-ee)—possibly fictional leader of Islamic State of Iraq.

Nicholas Berg—American radio-tower repairman beheaded by Abu Musab al-Zarqawi.

George W. Bush—forty-third President of the United States.

James Foley—American journalist beheaded by the Islamic State.

Abu Muhammad al-Julani (AH-boo moo-HAH-mahd joo-LAHN-ee)—leader and emir of al-Nusra Front.

Osama bin Laden (o-SAH-mah bin-LAH-duhn)—Saudi-born leader of al-Qaeda from 1989 to 2011.

Abu Muhammad al-Maqdisi (AH-boo moo-HAH-mahd al-mak-DIZ-ee)—militant Salafist cleric; religious mentor of Abu Musab al-Zarqawi.

Abu Ayyub al-Masri (AH-boo ah-YOOB al-MAHSS-ree)—leader of al-Qaeda in Iraq from 2006 to 2010.

Nouri al-Maliki (NOOR-ee al-MAL-ih-kee)—Prime Minister of Iraq 2006 to 2014.

Sergio Vieira de Mello (SEH-zhee-oh vee-A-rah day MEH-loh)—third UN High Commissioner for Human Rights.

Barack Obama—forty-fourth President of the United States.

Ray Odierno—American general; commander United States Forces–Iraq 2008 to 2010.

Leon Panetta—Director of the CIA 2009 to 2011.

David Petraeus—American general; commander of Multinational Force–Iraq 2007–2008.

Steven Sotloff—American journalist beheaded by the Islamic State.

Jack Straw—Foreign Secretary of Britain from 2001 to 2006.

Abu Kutaiba al-Urduni (AH-boo koo-TIE-buh al-er-DOON-ee)—Jordanian jihadi leader.

Andrew White—Anglican priest known as the "Vicar of Baghdad."

Ayman al-Zawahiri (EYE-mahn al-zah-WAH-ree)—current leader of al-Qaeda.

Abu Musab al-Zarqawi (AH-boo MOO-sahb al-zahr-KAW-wee)—militant Islamist from Jordan; founder of al-Qaeda in Iraq (AQI).

GLOSSARY

amnesty (AM-neh-stee)—general pardon, especially for offenses against a country or government

apostate (uh-POSS-tayt)—one who renounces one's religion, principles, or political party

bigoted (BIH-guh-tuhd)—unwilling to tolerate other people because of their ideas

caliph (KAY-lif or KAL-lif)—chief Muslim civil and religious leader

coerce (coe-ERSS)—obtain something by using force or the threat of force

depravity (di-PRAV-ih-tee)—moral corruption, wickedness

disavowal (diss-uh-VOW-al)—disclaimed knowledge or connection of something or someone

distraught (dih-STRAWT)—extremely upset

emir (eh-MEER)—title of various Muslim rulers

genocide (JEN-oh-side)—deliberate extermination of a race of people

ideology (ih-dee-OHL-o-gee)—the principal ideas or beliefs that characterize a particular class, group, or movement

insurgency (in-SUHR-juhn-cee)—revolt against an established government

Islam (IS-lahm, or is-LAHM)—the Muslim religion, based on the teachings of Muhammad; the Muslim world

jihad (jih-HAHD)—Arabic for to strive or struggle (in the path of God); holy war

manifesto (man-ih-FES-toh)—a public declaration of principles and policy

martyr (MAHR-tihr)—one who undergoes death or great suffering in support of a belief or cause or principle

monotheism (MAHN-oh-THEE-iz-ehm)—the belief that there is only one God

Muhammad (moo-HAH-mahd)—The Prophet; the founder of Islam

primeval (pry-MEE-vuhl)—the earliest ages in world history

profane (proh-FANE)—disrespectful of religious practice

Quran (kuh-RAN)—sacred book of Muslims containing the revelations of Muhammad

Salafism (sah-lah-FIHZ-em)—doctrine of militant Salafists who seek to restore Islam to their interpretation of its ideal, pristine form

Sharia (shuh-REE-uh)—legal and moral code of Islam

Shia (SHEE-uh)—the branch of Islam that regards Ali as the first successor of Muhammad; about 15 percent of Muslims worldwide are Shia

Sunni (SUUN-nee)—the branch of Islam that acknowledges the first four caliphs as rightful successors of Muhammad; about 85 percent of Muslims worldwide are Sunnis

FURTHER READING

Casil, Amy Sterling. *Coping with Terrorism*. New York: Rosen Publishing, 2004.
Englar, Mary. *September 11*. North Mankato, MN: Capstone Press, 2007.
Landau, Elaine. *Osama bin Laden: The Life and Death of the 9/11 al-Qaeda Mastermind*. Minneapolis, MN: Twenty-First Century Books, 2011.
Weinberg, Leonard. *Global Terrorism*. New York: Rosen Publishing, 2009.
Zahler, Kathy A. *The Assads' Syria*. Dictatorships Series. rev. ed. Minneapolis, MN: Twenty-First Century Books, 2012.

WORKS CONSULTED

"Al-Qaeda says new leader 'beheaded' kidnapped US soldiers." *The Scotsman*. June 17, 2006. http://www.scotsman.com/news/world/al-qaeda-says-new-leader-beheaded-kidnapped-us-soldiers-1-1122725
Andress, Carter, with Malcolm McConnell. *Victory Undone: The Defeat of al-Qaeda in Iraq and Its Resurrection as ISIS*. Washington, DC: Regnery Publishing, 2014.
Andrews, Mark. "Before Beheading, Children Tell ISIS: 'No, We Love Jesus'." *Charisma News*. December 2, 2014. http://www.charismanews.com/world/46330-before-beheading-children-tell-isis-no-we-love-jesus
Atwan, Abdel Bari. *The Secret History of al Qaeda*. Berkeley: University of California Press, 2006.
Burke, Jason. *Al-Qaeda: The True Story of Radical Islam*. 3rd ed. New York: Penguin Books, 2007.
Campo, Juan E., ed. *Encyclopedia of Islam*. New York: Checkmark Books, 2009.
Charles River Editors. *The Islamic State of Iraq and Syria: The History of ISIS/ISIL*. Cambridge, MA: Charles River Editors, 2014.
Hayes, Jonathan. "Second Opinion: A New York City medical examiner watches the video of Nick Berg's beheading and wishes he'd looked away." *New York* Magazine. May 31, 2004. http://nymag.com/nymetro/news/columns/witness/9183/
Kukis, Mark. "Bracing for an al-Qaeda Comeback." *TIME*. November 7, 2007. http://content.time.com/time/world/article/0,8599,1681443,00.html
Lister, Charles. "Profiling the Islamic State." Brookings Doha Center Analysis Paper. Number 13, November 2014. https://www.brookings.edu/wp-content/uploads/2014/12/en_web_lister.pdf
"Muslims React to Islamic State's Declaration of a Caliphate." *Christian-Muslim News Digest*. Issue 1(22) 2014. http://nifcon.anglicancommunion.org/media/110070/NIFCON-Digest-1-2014.pdf
Page, Susan. "Panetta: '30-year war' and a leadership test for Obama." *USA TODAY*. October 6, 2014. http://www.usatoday.com/story/news/politics/2014/10/06/leon-panetta-memoir-worthy-fights/16737615/
Pool, Jeffrey, trans. "Zarqawi's Pledge of Allegiance to al-Qaeda: From Mu'asker al-Battar, Issue 21." *Terrorism Monitor*, Volume: 2, Issue: 24. December 15, 2004. http://www.jamestown.org/single/?tx_ttnews%5Btt_news%5D=27305

WORKS CONSULTED

Raphaell, Nimrod. "'The Sheikh of the Slaughterers': Abu Mus'ab Al-Zarqawi and the Al-Qaeda Connection." MEMRI. Inquiry & Analysis Series Report No. 231. July 1, 2005. http://www.memri.org/report/en/0/0/0/0/0/0/1406.htm

Rosen, Nir. "Iraq's Jordanian Jihadis." *The New York Times*. February 19, 2006. http://www.nytimes.com/2006/02/19/magazine/iraq.html?pagewanted=all&_r=0

Sekulow, Jay, with Jordan Sekulow, Robert W. Ash, and David French. *The Rise of ISIS: A Threat We Can't Ignore*. New York: Howard Books, 2014.

"Seeds of al-Zarqawi army sown during prison term." *Lubbock Avalanche-Journal*. January 10, 2005. http://lubbockonline.com/stories/011005/wor_011005066.shtml

Sela, Avraham. *The Continuum Political Encyclopedia of the Middle East*. Revised and Updated Ed. New York: Continuum, 2002.

Sharp, Andrew. *The Rise of ISIS: The West's New Crusade*. San Bernardino, CA: Fusion Publications, 2014.

Spark, Joseph. *ISIS: Taking Over the Middle East: The Rise of Middle Eastern Supremacy ISIS/ISIL*. San Bernardo, CA: Conceptual Kings, 2014.

"Timeline: How Islamic State put itself on a collision course with the West." *ABC News*, October 3, 2014. http://www.abc.net.au/news/2014-10-03/islamic-state-a-timeline-of-escalating-terror/5788816

"Truck bomb kills chief U.N. envoy to Iraq." *CNN*. August 20, 2003. http://www.cnn.com/2003/WORLD/meast/08/19/sprj.irq.main

"Up to 40 die in Baghdad attacks." *The Guardian*. October 27, 2003. http://www.theguardian.com/world/2003/oct/27/iraq

Warrick, Joby. "ISIS, with gains in Iraq, close in on founder Zarqawi's violent vision." *The Washington Post*. June 14, 2014. https://www.washingtonpost.com/world/national-security/isiss-gains-in-iraq-fulfill-founders-violent-vision/2014/06/14/921ff6d2-f3b5-11e3-914c-1fbd0614e2d4_story.html?utm_term=.3b632d52374d

Weaver, Mary Anne. "The Short, Violent Life of Abu Musab al-Zarqawi." *The Atlantic*. Edited for the Web. June 8, 2006. http://www.theatlantic.com/magazine/archive/2006/07/the-short-violent-life-of-abu-musab-al-zarqawi/304983/

ON THE INTERNET

Bender, Jeremy. "As ISIS Routs The Iraqi Army, Here's A Look At What The Jihadists Have In Their Arsenal." *Business Insider*. July 8, 2014. http://www.businessinsider.com/isis-military-equipment-breakdown-2014-7?op=1

Ghosh, Bobby. "Roots of Evil: A short political history of the terrorists who call themselves the 'Islamic State.' " *Quartz*. August 14, 2014. http://qz.com/248787/a-short-political-history-of-the-barbaric-terrorists-who-call-themselves-the-islamic-state/

Laub, Zachary, and Jonathan Masters. "CFR Backgrounders: Islamic State in Iraq and Syria." Council on Foreign Relations. August 8, 2014. http://www.cfr.org/iraq/islamic-state-iraq-syria/p14811

INDEX